Ferenc Margitics - Erika Figula - Zsuzsa
Pauwlik

THE VICTIM
AND
BULLY-VICTIM

Background Factors of School
Bullying Behaviour

The Victim and Bully-Victim /Background Factors of School Bullying Behaviour/

Authored by: Ferenc Margitics PhD., Erika Figula PhD., Zsuzsa Pauwlik PhD.
(margitics.ferenc@nye.hu)
Edited and published by: Ervin K. Kery
(editor@kery.org)

ISBN: 9781708412739

CONTENTS

Preface

Our research group established by the Department of Psychology at the College of Nyíregyháza investigates the phenomena of school bullying and harassment. The term 'school bullying covers the behaviour where the aggressive act has no obvious cause (non-reactive aggression).

Our research focuses on the question that among upper school primary school students and high school students what kind of background factors may stand in the background of aggressive attitude and behavior patterns of school bullying (bully, victim, bystander, intervener participant and helper participant). During our research, we charted those background factors, which help to understand the process of the development of bully, victim, participant and bystander behavior patterns, as well as they allow the development of the options of efficient mental hygiene.

In this book we examined the relation between **victim or bully-victim behavior patterns** in school bullying and certain parental treatments (such as; parental solicitude, parental overprotection and parental restriction). We wanted to find an answer to the question: what kind of temperament and character traits the students have, who become victim or bully victim through school bullying and what their typical emotional reactions are.

In our research we used the following instruments: the Questionnaire on School Bullying, the Hungarian adaptation of Goch's Family Socializational, the Hungarian adaptation of the Parental Bonding Instrument, the Hungarian version of Cloninger's Temperament and Character Inventory, the Hungarian version of Differential Emotions Scale, The Hungarian version of Weismann's Scale of Dysfunctional Attitudes and The Hungarian adaptation of the Folkman–Lazarus Conflict Solving Questionnaire.

Introduction

School bullying is not an isolated problem unique to specific cultures, but is prevalent worldwide, as evidenced by a large international research base. (Eslea et al., 2004; Cook et al., 2009).

The research results show (Smith et al., 1999), that the victims of bullying are in minority (approximately 5-20% of the children and the harassers (who injured the others) are usually even less (about 2-20%).

The some 14% of the students in elementary and lower secondary schools (grades 4–10), roughly corresponding to ages 9–16) in Norway are involved in bully/victim problems with some regularity in 2010 – either as pure bullies, pure victims, or bully-victims (Olweus 2010).

School bullying is observed as early as in preschool and generally peaks during middle school (around ages 11 through 14) and somewhat decreases toward the end of high school (Hymel and Swearer 2015).

According to our research in Hungarian primary and secondary school from the reactions on school bullying, victim behavior pattern was the least typical of the sample. At the age of 11-12, both the girls and the boys became victims of school bullying approximately at the same level. From the age of 13-14, we found this behavior pattern more typical of girls, which was not significant in the case of either of the age groups. Examining the individual components of victim behavior pattern, the situation was different. In case of affective reaction (emotional effect of the insult) we find significant differences in all age groups, the girls seem to be more liable to it than the boys. The primary school boys seemed to be more liable to physical reaction (bodily reaction to the insult) than the girls. This kind of inclination was more typical of the high school boys but at this age, it was not so significant. Claim for social support (refusal in the class community) was also more typical of boys but this difference was significant in case of 15-16 year old boys. We cannot demonstrate important differences in the case of cognitive (apperception and assimilation of the insult). (Margitics et. al, 2019).

According to Kathleen (2007), there should be personality traits or behavior patterns, which bring about that certain students are more likely to become the victims of other students' attacks.

On the one hand, Giesekus (2002) sees those students as victims, who are attacked without their resistance; on the other hand according to him, those students are victims who are randomly selected and attacked and they are purposefully harassed again and again.

Olweus (1995) divides up the group of victims into two subgroups: passive victims (pure victims) and provocative victims (bully-victims). Most of the victims can be classified into the group of passive victims. According to Giesekus (2002), passive victims are those victims who are attacked without resistance.

According to Rost (1998), passive victims are unconfident and shy.

The pure or passive victims are usually more anxious and insecure than students in general. They are often cautious, sensitive, and quiet. When attacked by other students, they may react by withdrawal. The victims suffer from low self-esteem and have a negative view of themselves and their situation. The victims are lonely at school. As a rule, they do not have a single good friend in their classroom. They are not aggressive or teasing in their behavior. (Olweus, 1978).

The pure victims signal to their peers that they are insecure and worthless individuals who will not retaliate if they are attacked or insulted. Such children may be perceived to be "easy marks" by dominant, aggressive peers and are thus at increased risk of being victimized.

Olweus (1993) demonstrated in general that passive victims approach themselves negatively, they see themselves as losers, they do not consider themselves attractive, and they are often ashamed of themselves.

The pure victims of bullying often experience loneliness and internalizing issues (e.g., anxiety, depression), and low self-esteem (Swearer and Hymel, 2015).

Olweus' depth interviews with the mothers indicated that those children, who have become passive victims of bullying, were characterized by a certain caution and sensitivity at an early age. Overall, the behavior of the passive types indicates to their environment that they feel themselves uncertain and worthless and when they are attacked or hurt by others, they will not attack (Olweus, 1997).

Margitics et al. (2010) found that those temperament type students can become pure victims through school bullying, who avoid something by necessity (systematic, objective, detached even so they have low self-validation) and they are characterized by low novelty seeking and reward dependence and high harm avoidance.

The pure victims are at clearly increased risk of developing various forms of internalizing problems such as depression, anxiety, and poor self-esteem. (Hawker and Boulton, 2000).

Bully-victims, children who bully others and are also victimized themselves, have attracted increasing attention by researchers during the past decades (Schwartz, 2000; Solberg et al., 2007).

Bully-victims are often considered a subtype of bullies, sometimes called reactive bullies, and are seldom discussed under the characteristics of victims (Volk et al. 2012).

Bully-victims are a much smaller group than pure bullies or pure victims, and they are especially rare among girls. They are a distinct subgroup when it comes to forms of bullying and victimization. (Yang and Salmivalli, 2013).

Bully-victims are group with prevalence rates ranging from 1% to 12% (Hymel and Swearer 2015).

The bully-victims show a distinct pattern from pure bullies and pure victims with respect to the forms of bullying they employ and experience. (Yang and Salmivalli, 2013).

According Yang and Salmivalli (2013) research bully-victims differed from pure bullies most clearly in employing higher levels verbal and physical bullying.

Bully-victims often hurt others while he/she is also the victim of attacks. In his/her case, reactive aggression is typical because they react to the innocent, accidental or real insults in the same way.

In contrast with passive victims, according to Olweus (1995), provocative or bully-victims are not only shy but they show aggressive behavior. They seem to be ready to attack, their confusing behavior creates tension and with this they arouse negative reactions from their peers. It is common that they have concentration problems.

For Giesekus (2002), bully-victims victims are those students, who react angrily earlier than the average and they are not able to resolve stress associated with conflicts. These children more often become victims of others' aggression and they react more shyly, aggressively and intensely.

The bully-victims or provocative victims are characterized by a combination of anxious and aggressive reaction patterns and have characteristics in common with both pure victims and pure bullies. The bully-victims resemble the pure victims in being depressive and anxious with poor global self-esteem and feeling disliked by peers. On the other hand, the provocative victims also show similarities with pure bullies by having elevated levels of dominant, aggressive, and antisocial behavior and may in addition have problems with concentration, hyperactivity, and impulsivity. (Olweus and Breivik, 2014).

Results of different studies suggest that these children are more at risk of developing psychological difficulties than either pure bullies or pure victims (Duncan, 1999; Wolke et al, 2000).

The bully-victims suffer from more frequent victimization than pure victims, and that they are attacked in multiple ways. A plausible explanation is their rejection and lack of friends. The bully-victims might be more easily seen as "deserving" their negative treatment, due to their own disturbing behaviour. (Yang and Salmivalli, 2013).

Bully-victims are often described as emotionally dysregulated, hot-tempered, and high on reactive aggression (Salmivalli and Nieminen, 2002)

According to Margitics and his colleagues (2010) researches, the borderline temperament type students, who can be characterized by high novelty seeking, harm avoidance and low reward dependence, are the typical bully-victims of school bullying. Uncertainty of mood, low performance and inability to make decisions are typical of them. Passive-aggressive temperament type students (uncertainty, shrillness, manipulative attitude), who are characterized by high novelty seeking, harm avoidance and reward dependence, can be also provocative victims. Excitable (dependence) students, who are characterized by low self-directedness, self-transcendence experience and high cooperativeness, can become bully-victims. This character type is submissive, optimistic, respectful to others but sensitive to criticism and insult, excitable.

Lereya, Samara and Wolke (2013) looked at victim or bully-victim roles. Warm and authoritative parenting appeared as a protective factor. Abuse and neglect appeared as a risk factor, very strongly so for bully/victims. Overprotection is another risk factor for being a victim.

METHODOLOGY

Participants

Factors of Family Socialization

In the study 647 (301 girls, 346 boys) primary and high school students took part. The distribution of the sample according to schools was the following:

> ➢ Primary school, upper school: 293 participants (140 girls, 150 boys)
> ➢ High school: 354 participants (161 girls, 193 boys)

The sample according to age:

> ➢ Primary school, upper school: 13,2 year old
> ➢ High school: 16,7 year old

Temperament and Character

The data for the research project were gathered from students of secondary grammar schools.

341 students participated in the project,

195 women and 146 men.

The average age was 16,4 years (standard deviation: 1,4).

Emotions, Attitudes and Coping Mechanisms

The data for the research project were gathered from students of primary education at elementary schools and secondary grammar schools.

706 students participated in the project, 397 women and 309 men.

The average age was 15,2 years (standard deviation: 1,7).

Measures

Factors of Family Socialization

We applied two different questionnaires.

The Hungarian adaptation of Goch's Family Socializational Questionnaire (Goch, 1998, Sallay and Dabert, 2002).

The questionnaire describes the following dimensions of family socialization:

> type of the family atmosphere (rule-oriented family atmosphere, conflict-oriented family atmosphere),
> breeding target (breeding for autonomy, autonomy as a target of breeding, breeding for conformity, conformity as a breeding target),
> educational attitudes (consistent educational attitude, manipulative educational attitude, inconsistent educational attitude)
> educational style (supporting educational style, punishing educational style).

The Hungarian adaptation of the Parental Bonding Instrument (Tóth and Gervai, 1999).

The questionnaire has three main scales: love and care, overprotection, and restriction, applied separately to the mother and the father.

Temperament and Character

The Hungarian version of Cloninger's Temperament and Character Inventory (Rózsa et al. 2005)

The main scales of the measure describe four temperament and three character dimensions:

> ➤ The temperament-scales are novelty seeking, harm avoidance, reward dependence, persistence

> ➤ The character-scales are self-directedness, cooperativeness, self-transcendence.

Emotions

Hungarian version of Differentional Emotions Scale (Oláh, 2005).

Izard (1971) developed Differential Emotions Scale in order to differentiate between the basic emotions. The inventory is suitable for examining the ability of experiencing certain basic emotions as a permanent characteristic feature.

With the help of a frequency scale it examines how often the basic emotions appear.

Differential Emotions Scale consists of a scale identifying ten basic emotions. The questionnaire describes the following fundamental emotions:

- ➢ Trait of Interest
- ➢ Trait of Enjoyment
- ➢ Trait of Surprise
- ➢ Trait of Distress
- ➢ Trait of Anger
- ➢ Trait of Disgust
- ➢ Trait of Contempt
- ➢ Trait of Fear
- ➢ Trait of Shame
- ➢ Trait of Guilt
- ➢ Trait of Anxiety

The Hungarian adaptation of the questionnaire was done by Oláh (2005), who found the reliability of the scales good (Cronbach-alpha=0,49-0,76).

Attitudes

The Hungarian version of Weismann's Scale of Dysfunctional Attitudes (Weisman and Beck, 1979, Kopp, 1994).

The scale included question of following attitudes:

> desire for external appraisal, need for affections, performance orientation, perfectionism, rightful and intensive requirements towards the environment, omnipotence (intensive altruism) and external control - autonomy.

Coping Mechanisms

The Hungarian adaptation of the Folkman–Lazarus Conflict Solving Questionnaire (Kopp, 1994).

The questionnaire contains 22 items and is used to reveal the behaviour of individuals in difficult situations. Respondents use a four-grade scale for each answer, from "entirely irrelevant" to "fully relevant."

Folkman and Lazarus arranged

conflict-solving strategies into problem-based and emotion-based categories. The surveys conducted by Kopp and Skrabski (1995) confirmed the validity of this categorization. They found three problem-driven, three emotion-driven and one support-seeking factor. These are the following:

> Problem analysis
> Cognitive restructuring
> Conformance
> Emotion-driven action
> Seeking emotional balance
> Retrieval
> Call for help
> A summary indicator of the problem-driven coping strategy
> A summary indicator of the emotion-driven coping strategy

Problem-driven coping strategies (problem analysis, cognitive re-structuring, conformance) measure the ability of the individual to analyse the problem, to influence the reasons and to obtain control over it. It also measures the ability of cognitive re-structuring.

The second three emotion-driven

coping strategies (emotion-driven action, seeking emotional equilibrium, retrieval) and call for help will come forward when the individual is not satisfactorily familiar with the problem or feels unable to obtain control over the situation.

The Examination of School Bullying

The Questionnaire on School Bullying (Figula et al., 2019).

For purposes of identifying patterns of behaviour in school bullying, the School Bullying Questionnaire was used.

The 70 items of SBQ offers options of "almost never," "sometimes," "often," "almost always," and investigates the phenomena of school bullying and abuse in everyday life through five dimensions.

Scales and Subscales	Item	Cronbach-alfa
Victim Scale	**33**	**0,847**
Cognitive Subscale (Conscious recognition of abuse and processing it)	15	0,877
Affective Subscale (The emotional effect of	12	0,864

abuse)		
Somatic reaction (Somatic reaction to abuse / acting out)	3	0,758
Lack of Social Support Subscale (Lack of acceptance in class community)	3	0,814
Intervener Participant Scale	**3**	**0,784**
Helper Participant Scale	**8**	**0,753**
Intervening to Pacify Subscale	3	0,748
Intervening to Ask for Help Subscale	2	0,778
Affective Subscale (Inner tension as a result of witnessing aggression)	3	0,749
Bystander Scale	**9**	**0,768**
Keeping Distance Subscale	6	0,758
Fear Subscale	3	0,743
Bully Scale	**17**	**0,843**
Physical Aggression Subscale	4	0,845
Verbal Aggression Subscale	5	0,849
Exclusion Subscale	5	0,754
Advantage From Attack Subscale	3	0,768

Chart 1. Scales and Subscales of the School Bullying Questionnaire

With the exception of "intervener participant" scale, all dimensions include further subscales. (Chart 1).

The Criteria of Compiling the Research Group and the Control Group

When we formed the test groups, we considered the results scored on the scales of Questionnaire on School Bullying, which examines the behavior patterns of school bullying, within this, which quartiles the tested people got into.

Those students got into the group of students becoming victim during school bullying, who fell into the fourth quartile of the sample on the basis of the results scored on the Victim Scale as well as they scored average or less than average values on the Bully Scale.

Those students got into the group of students not becoming victim during school bullying, who fell into the first quartile of the sample on the basis of the results scored on the Victim Scale as well as they scored average or less than average values on the Bully Scale.

Those students got into the group of students becoming bully-victims during school bullying, who fell into the fourth quartile on the basis of the results scored on both the Bully Scale and the Victim Scale.

Those students got into the group of students not becoming bully-victims during school bullying, who fell into the first quartile on the basis of the results scored on both the Bully Scale and the Victim Scale.

Results

Factors of Family Socialization

The structure of Family Socialization factors

With the help of second-rate factor analysis (varimax rotation) we examined the patterns of parental educational dimensions, its underlying structure (during the study- according to general practice- not less than 0,4 (factor gravity) rotated factors were taken into account (Chart 2).

Dimensions of Parental Bonding	Factor 1	Factor 2	Factor 3	Factor 4
Rule oriented family atmosphere r	0,641			
Conflict oriented family atmosphere		0,730		
Manipulative educational attitude		0,670		
Inconsistent educational attitude		0,758		

Consistent educational attitude	**0,662**		
Punishing educational style	**0,772**		
Supportive educational style			**-0,469**
Breeding for conformity	**0,759**		
Breeding for autonomy			**-0,619**
Maternal affection-care		**-0,595**	
Paternal affection-care		**-0,648**	
Maternal overprotection				**0,854**
Paternal overprotection				**0,878**
Maternal restriction			**0,898**	
Paternal restriction			**0,895**	

Chart 2. Second Rate Factor Analysis for the Dimensions of Parental Nurturing (l>0.4)

The analysis arranged parental educational dimension into four factors, which together explained 64,9% of the variance.

The first factor, which explains 25,2% of the variance, demonstrates rule oriented family atmosphere, which is characterized by conformity as parental educational goal and it associates with punishing educational style and consistent educational attitude.

The second factor, which explains 21,4% of the variance, demonstrates conflict oriented family atmosphere, which is characterized by conflict oriented family atmosphere, the manipulative and inconsistent educational attitude of the parents and the lack of love and care.

The third factor, which explains 10,6% of the variance, demonstrates restrictional parental treatment, which is characterized by the lack of parental support and breeding for autonomy

The fourth factor, which explains 7,7%of the variance, describes parental overprotection.

The connection between victim and provocative victim behavior patterns of school bullying and parental educational effects were revealed by linear regression analysis (stepwise method: dependant variable was the victim or bully-victim behavior patterns of school bullying, parental educational effects were used as predictor).

Chart 3 shows the results of linear regression analysis in case of victim behavior pattern.

Predictor	B	t	P<
Women: $F_{totál}$=16,972; df=3/301; p<0,000			
Conflict oriented family atmosphere	0,234	3,933	0,000
Manipulative educational attitude	0,211	3,159	0,001
Rule oriented family atmosphere	0,173	3,191	0,002
Men: $F_{totál}$=21,438; df=4/346; p<0,000			
Manipulative educational attitude	0,265	4,124	0,000
Conflict oriented family atmosphere	0,210	3,980	0,000
Maternal overprotection	0,189	3,123	0,001
Rule oriented family atmosphere	0,165	2,987	0,003

Chart 3. Interrelationship between Parental Rearing Effects with the Behaviour Patterns of the Victim (approved models; p<0.05)

In case of the girls, victim behavior pattern, from the parental educational effects, showed a significant, positive connection with conflict oriented family atmosphere, rule oriented family atmosphere and manipulative educational attitude, which together explained 16,7% of the variance of victim behavior pattern.

In case of the boys, victim behavior pattern, from the parental educational effects, showed a significant, positive connection with conflict oriented family atmosphere, manipulative educational attitude, parental overprotection and rule oriented family atmosphere, which together explained 17,9% of the variance of victim behavior pattern.

Chart 4 shows the results of linear regression analysis in case of bully-victim behavior pattern.

Predictor	B	t	P<
Women: $F_{totál}$=28,156; df=4/301; p<0,000			
Maternal affection-care	-0,221	-3,764	0,000
Paternal affection-care	-0,205	-3,452	0,000
Conflict oriented family atmosphere	0,185	3,025	0,001
Manipulative educational attitude	0,177	2,987	0,003
Men: $F_{totál}$=17,654; df=4/346; p<0,000			
Paternal	0,234	3,912	0,000

overprotection			
Maternal overprotection	0,201	3,401	0,000
Paternal affection-care	-0,189	-3,054	0,001
Conflict oriented family atmosphere	0,162	2,548	0,008

Chart 4. Interrelationship between Parental Rearing Effects with the Behaviour Patterns of the Bully-Victim (approved models; p<0.05)

In case of the girls, bully-victim behavior pattern, from the parental educational effects, showed a significant, negative connection with maternal and paternal affection-care and a positive one with maternal overprotection and conflict oriented family atmosphere, which together explained 22,7% of the variance of bully-victim behavior pattern.

In case of the boys, bully-victim behavior pattern, from the parental educational effects, showed a significant, positive connection with paternal and maternal overprotection, conflict oriented family atmosphere and a negative one with paternal affection-care, which together explained 26,7% of the variance of bully-victim behavior pattern.

Temperament and Character

We examined what differences exist between the test groups (victim vs. non-victim, bully-victim vs. non bully-victim) on the basis of the results scored on the Bully and Victim Scales of the Questionnaire on School Bullying examining the behavior patterns of school bullying.

Figure 1 shows the averages scored on the certain scales of Temperament and Character Inventory of victim vs. non-victim test groups in case of the girls.

In case of the girls, both in the areas of temperament traits and character traits, we found significant differences between the test groups on the basis of Comparative Statistical Analysis (two-sample t-test).

We find significant differences between the test groups, from the certain temperament traits, in case of harm avoidance and reward dependence.

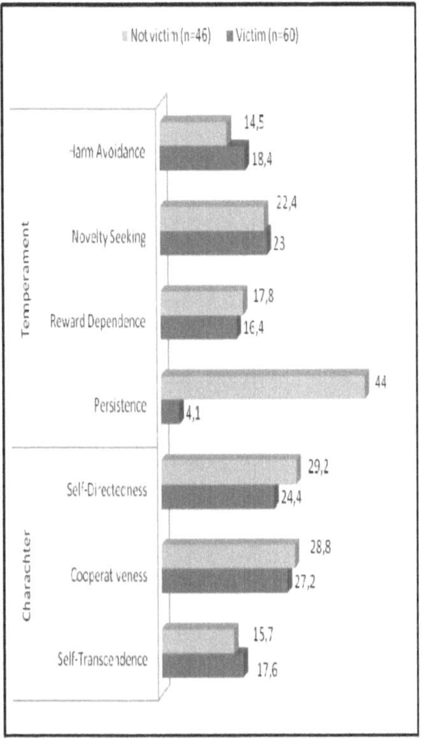

Figure 1. Averages Achieved on the Individual Scales of the Temperament and Character Inventory by Victim Test Group vs. Non-Victim Test Group (girls)

We found harm avoidance more typical of the girls, who become victims of school bullying (t=3,986, p<0,001), and reward dependence more typical of girls, who do not become victims (t=3,012, p<0,05).

From the character traits, only in the area of self-directedness was a significant difference between the groups. Self-directedness was more typical of the girls not becoming victims (t=4,608, p<0,001), than the girls becoming victims.

Figure 2 shows the averages scored on the certain scales of Temperament and Character Inventory of victim vs. non-victim control groups in case of the boys.

In case of the boys, only in one area of temperament and character traits, we found significant differences between the victim and not victim test groups on the basis of Comparative Statistical Analysis

The temperament of the boys becoming victims of school bullying is more harm-avoiding (t=4,371, p<0,001), the character of them is less self-directed (t=5,192, p<0,001), than the temperament and character of the boys not becoming victims of school bullying.

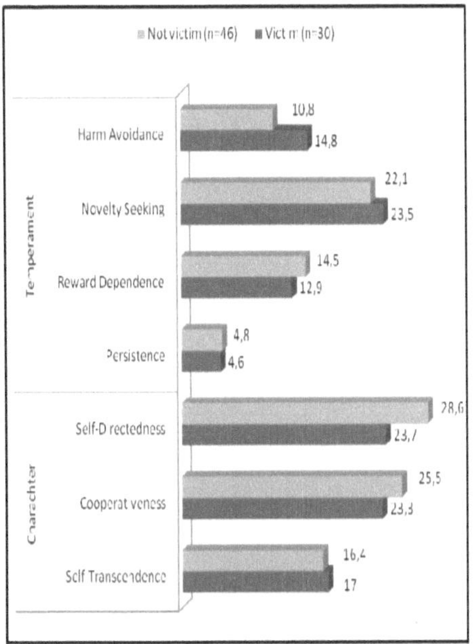

Figure 2. Averages Achieved on the Individual Scales of the Temperament and Character Inventory by Victim Test Group vs. Non-Victim Test Group (boys)

Figure 3 shows the averages scored on the certain scales of Temperament and Character Inventory of bully-victim vs. non bully-victim test groups in case of the girls.

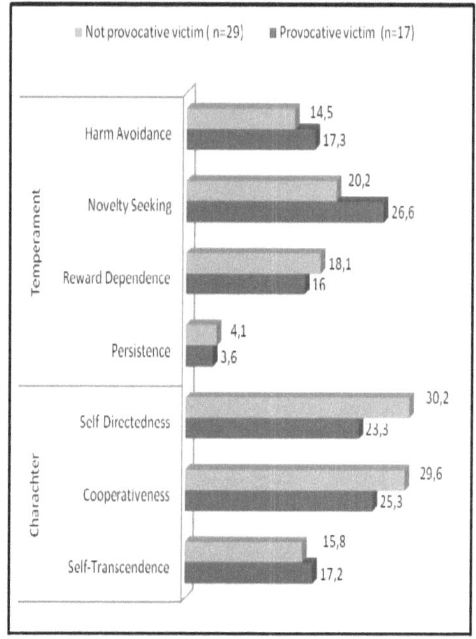

Figure 3. Averages Achieved on the Individual Scales of the Temperament and Character Inventory by Bully-Victim Test Group vs. Non Bully-Victim Test Group (girls)

In case of the girls, on the basis of Comparative Statistical Analysis we found significant differences in point of temperament traits, in case of novelty seeking and reward dependence, in point of character traits, in case of cooperativeness and self-directedness between the bully-victim and non bully-victim test groups.

We found novelty seeking (t=3,859, p<0,01) and reward dependence (t=3,291, p<0,05), more typical of the girls becoming bully-victims of school bullying, cooperativeness (t=3,131, p<0,05) and self-directedness (t=5,335, p<0,001were more typical of the girls not becoming bully-victims.

Figure 4 shows the averages scored on the certain scales of Temperament and Character Inventory of bully-victim vs. non bully-victim control groups in case of the boys.

In case of the boys, on the basis of Comparative Statistical Analysis, we found significant differences in point of temperament traits, in case of harm avoidance and reward dependence, in point of character traits, in case of cooperativeness and self-directedness between the bully-victim and not bully-victim control groups.

We found reward dependence (t=3,671, p<0,01) and harm avoidance (t=3,713, p<0,01), more typical of the boys becoming bully-victims of school bullying, cooperativeness (t=3,213, p<0,05) and self-directedness (t=4,478, p<0,001), were more typical of the boys not becoming bully-victims.

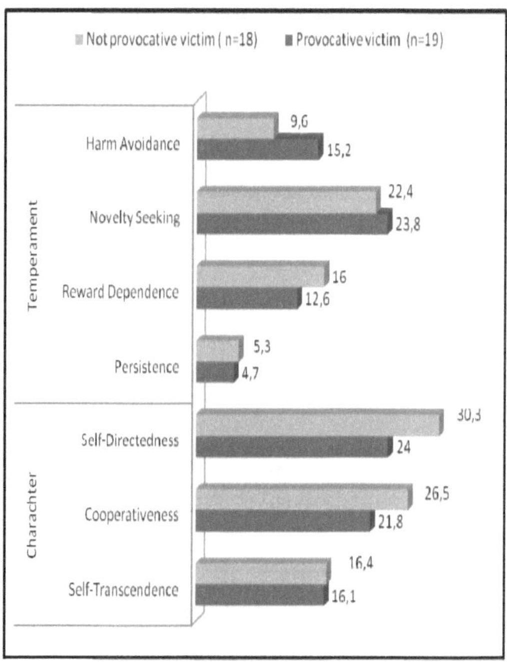

Figure 4. Averages Achieved on the Individual Scales of the Temperament and Character Inventory by Bully-Victim Test Group vs. Non Bully-Victim Test Group (boys)

The connection between victim or bully-victim behavior patterns of school bullying and temperament and character traits were revealed by linear regression analysis (stepwise method: dependant variable was the behavior patterns of school bullying, independent variables were the certain temperament and character traits and their constituent personality traits.

Chart 5 shows the results of linear regression analysis in case of victim behavior pattern.

Predictor	B	t	P<
Women: $F_{totál}$=9,360; df=4/195; p<0,000			
Self-Directedness	-0,239	-3,178	0,002
Dependence	-0,179	-2,598	0,010
Social acceptance	-0,178	-2,480	0,014
Harm-Avoidance	0,154	2,092	0,038
Men: $F_{totál}$=9,582; df=2/146; p<0,000			
Harm-Avoidance	0,244	3,065	0,003
Social acceptance	-0,211	-2,651	0,009

Chart 5. Correlation between Temperament and Character Features and the Behaviour Pattern of the Victim (approved models; p<0.05)

In case of the girls, victim behavior pattern, from the temperament an character traits and their constituent personality traits, showed a significant, negative connection with self-directness, other people's reward dependence and social acceptance and a positive one with harm avoidance, which together explained 19,8 % of the variance of victim behavior pattern.

In case of the boys, victim behavior pattern, from the temperament an character traits and their constituent personality traits, showed a significant, positive connection with harm avoidance and a negative one with social acceptance, which together explained 11,9 % of the variance of victim behavior pattern.

Predictor	B	t	P<
Women: $F_{totál}$=21,146; df=3/195; p<0,000			
Self-Directedness	-0,264	-4,048	0,000
Dependence	-0,238	-3,722	0,000
Social acceptance	-0,233	-3,517	0,001
Men: $F_{totál}$=7,116; df=3/146; p<0,000			
Purposefulness	-0,309	-3,334	0,001
Harm-Avoidance	0,265	3,001	0,003
Resourcefulness	0,195	2,012	0,046

Chart 6. Correlation between Temperament and Character Features and the Behaviour Pattern of the Bully-Victim (approved models; p<0.05)

Chart 6 shows the results of linear regression analysis in case of bully-victim behavior pattern.

In case of the girls, bully-victim behavior pattern, from the temperament and character traits and their constituent personality traits, showed a significant, negative connection with self-directedness, other people's reward dependence, social acceptance, which together explained 24,9 % of the variance of bully-victim behavior pattern.

In case of the boys, bully-victim behavior pattern, from the temperament and character traits and their constituent personality traits, showed a significant, positive connection with harm avoidance and a negative one with efficiency, resourcefulness, inventiveness, which together explained 13,1 % of the variance of bully-victim behavior pattern.

Emotions

We examined what difference exists between the test groups in point of basic emotions on the basis of the results scored on the scales of the victim behavior pattern Questionnaire on School Bullying

Figure 5 shows the averages scored on the certain scales of Differential Emotions Scale of victim vs. non-victim control groups in case of the girls.

Comparative Statistical Analysis (two-sample t-test) shows that there were significant differences between the test groups in point of more basic emotions.

These are the following:

➤ Shame (t=5,417, p<0,000)
➤ Fear (t=5,145, p<0,000)
➤ Contempt (t=3,396, p<0,001)
➤ Enjoyment (t=2,982, p<0,003)
➤ Guilt (t=2,603, p<0,010)
➤ Anger (t=2,150, p<0,033)

These results indicate that shame, fear, contempt, guilt and feeling anger were rather typical of the girls becoming victims of school bullying than the girls not becoming victims.

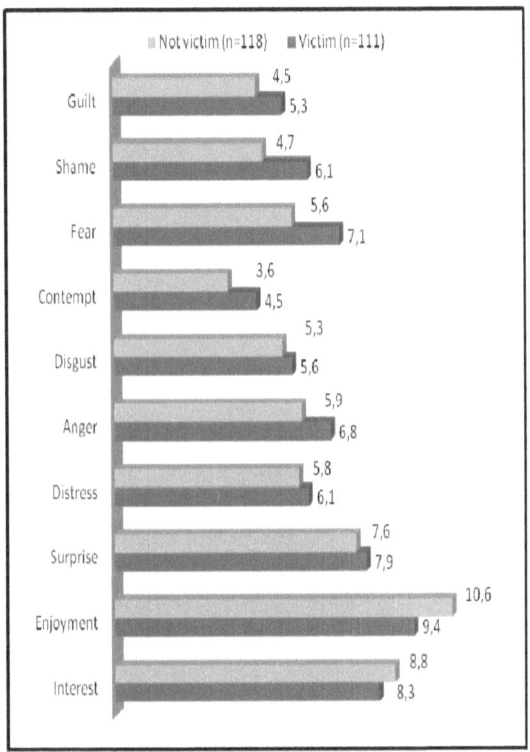

Figure 5. Achieved on the Individual Scales of the Differential Emotions Scale by Victim Test Group vs. Non-Victim Test Group (girls)

Figure 6 shows the averages scored on the certain scales of Differential Emotions Scale of victim vs. non-victim control groups in case of the boys.

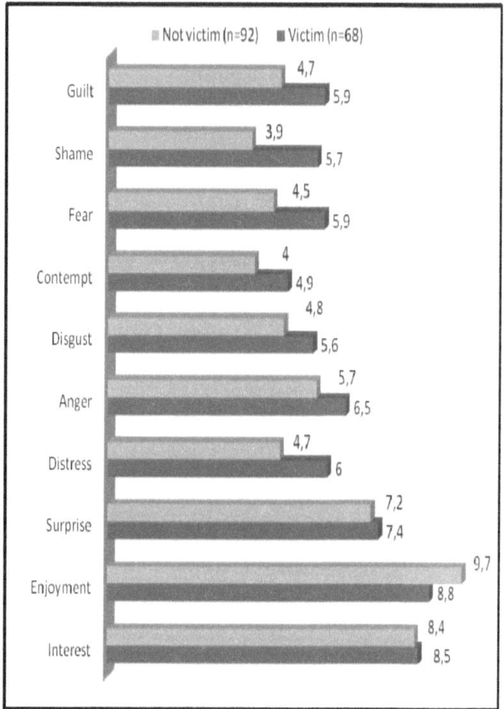

Figure 6. Averages Achieved on the Individual Scales of the Differential Emotions Scale by Victim Test Group vs. Non-Victim Test Group (boys)

Comparative Statistical Analysis shows that in case of the boys there were also significant differences between the test groups in point of more basic emotions.

These are the following:

- ➢ Shame (t=6,604, p<0,000)
- ➢ Fear (t=5,064, p<0,000)
- ➢ Guilt (t=4,226, p<0,000)
- ➢ Distress (t=3,984, p<0,000)
- ➢ Contempt (t=3,396, p<0,001)
- ➢ Disgust (t=3,337, p<0,001)
- ➢ Enjoyment (t=2,703, p<0,008)
- ➢ Anger (t=2,645, p<0,009)

These results indicate that shame, fear, guilt, distress, contempt, disgust and feeling anger were rather typical of the boys becoming victims of school bullying than the boys not becoming victims.

The connection between the victim behavior pattern of school bullying and the basic emotions were revealed by linear regression analysis (stepwise method: dependant variable was victim behavior pattern, basic emotions were used as predictors).

Chart 7 shows the results of linear regression analysis in case of victim behavior pattern.

Predictor	B	t	P<
Women: $F_{totál}=25,309$; df=2/397; p<0,000			
Fear	0,280	6,041	0,000
Contempt	0,218	4,700	0,000
Men: $F_{totál}=40,973$; df=2/309; p<0,000			
Shame	0,298	5,082	0,000
Fear	0,231	3,949	0,000

Chart 7. Relationship of Fundamental Emotions with the Behaviour Pattern of the Victim (approved models; p<0.05)

In case of the girls, victim behavior pattern, from the basic emotions, showed a significant, positive connection with fear and contempt, which together explained 16,2 % of the variance.

In case of the boys, victim behavior pattern, from the basic emotions, showed a significant, positive connection with also fear and shame, which together explained 21,1 % of the variance of victim behavior pattern.

These results indicate that the students becoming victims of school bullying – without reference to gender differences- feel fear, which associates with shame in case of the boys and contempt in case of the girls.

We also examined that what the connection is between the certain components of victim behavior pattern (cognitive, affective, physical reaction, lack of social support) and the basic emotions (linear regression, stepwise method: dependant variable is the components of victim behavior pattern, basic emotions were used as predictors).

Chart 8 shows the regression analysis of the basic emotions according to the components of victim behavior pattern.

Predictor	B	t	P<
Cognitive (apperception and assimilation of the insult)			
Women: $F_{totál}$=20,667; df=2/397; p<0,000			
Fear	0,240	5,004	0,000
Contempt	0,177	3,679	0,000
Men: $F_{totál}$=34,144; df=2/309; p<0,000			
Shame	0,299	5,017	0,000
Fear	0,190	3,177	0,002
Affective (emotional effect of the insult)			
Women: $F_{totál}$=24,617; df=2/397; p<0,000			
Fear	0,266	6,596	0,000
Contempt	0,172	3,511	0,000
Men: $F_{totál}$=45,153; df=2/309; p<0,000			
Fear	0,315	5,433	0,000
Shame	0,234	4,038	0,000
Physical reaction (bodily reaction to the insult)			
Women: $F_{totál}$=25,241; df=2/397; p<0,000			

Anger	0,277	5,413	0,000
Contempt	0,115	2,258	0,024
Men: $F_{totál}$=64,862; df=2/309; p<0,000			
Anger	0,477	8,514	0,000
Disgust	0,179	3,153	0,002
Shortage of social support (refusal in the class community)			
Women: $F_{totál}$=25,309; df=2/397; p<0,000			
Enjoyment	-0,207	-4,237	0,000
Shame	0,193	3,966	0,000
Men: $F_{totál}$=16,961; df=2/309; p<0,000			
Enjoyment	-0,230	-4,020	0,000
Distress	0,156	2,731	0,007

Chart 8. Regression Analysis of Fundamental Emotions versus the Individual Components of the Victim Behaviour Pattern (approved models; p<0.05)

In case of the girls, the cognitive component of victim behavior pattern, from the basic emotions, showed a significant, positive connection with fear and contempt, which together explained 9,5 % of the variance.

In case of the boys, the cognitive component of victim behavior pattern, from the basic emotions, showed a significant, positive connection with fear and shame, which together explained 18,2 % of the variance.

In case of the girls, the affective component of victim behavior pattern, from the basic emotions, showed a significant, positive connection with fear and contempt, which together explained 12,3 % of the variance.

In case of the boys, the affective component of victim behavior pattern, from the basic emotions, showed a significant, positive connection with fear and shame, which together explained 22,8 % of the variance.

In case of the girls, the physical reaction component of victim behavior pattern, from the basic emotions, showed a significant, positive connection with anger and contempt, which together explained 12,5 % of the variance.

In case of the boys, the physical reaction component of victim behavior pattern, from the basic emotions, showed a significant, positive connection with also anger and disgust, which together explained 29,8 % of the variance.

In case of the girls, the lack of social support component of victim behavior pattern, from the basic emotions, showed a significant, positive connection with shame and a negative one with enjoyment, which together explained 11 % of the variance.

In case of the boys, the lack of social support component of victim behavior pattern, from the basic emotions, showed a significant, positive connection with distress and a negative one with enjoyment, which together explained 10 % of the variance.

Attitudes

We examined what difference exists between the test groups in point of dysfunctional attitudes on the basis of the results scored on the victim scale of the behavior pattern Questionnaire on School Bullying

Figure 7 shows the averages scored on the certain scales of Scale of Dysfunctional Attitudes victim vs. non-victim test groups in case of the girls.

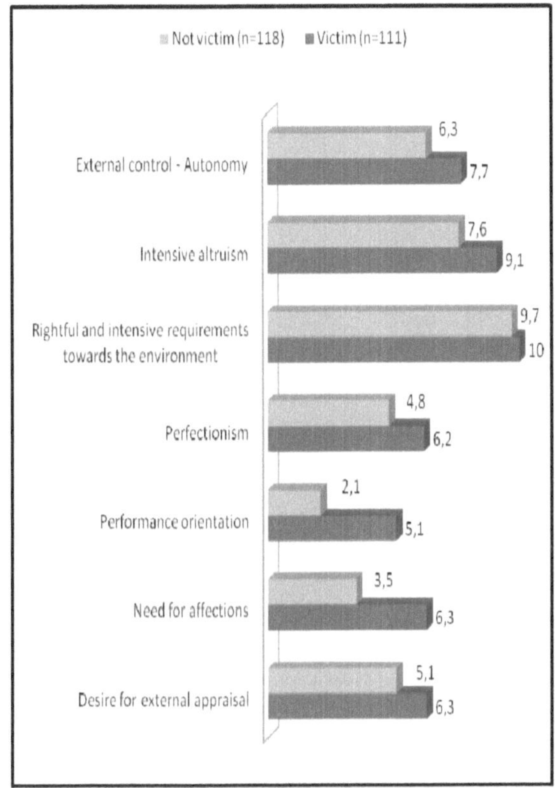

Figure 7. Averages Achieved on the Scale of Dysfunctional Attitudes by the Victim Test Group vs. Non-Victim Test Group (girls)

Comparative Statistical Analysis (two-sample t-test) shows that there were significant differences between the test groups in point of more dysfunctional attitudes.

These are the following:

> Performance orientation (t=4,989, p<0,000)
> Need for affections (t=4,780, p<0,000)
> Perfectionism (t=3,150, p<0,001)
> Intensive altruism (t=3,143, p<0,002)
> External control - Autonomy (t=3,090, p<0,002)
> Desire for external appraisal (t=2,587, p<0,010)

These results indicate that performance orientation, need for affections, perfectionism, intensive altruism, desire for external control and appraisal were rather typical of the girls becoming victims of school bullying than the girls not becoming victims.

Figure 8 shows the averages scored on the certain scales of Scale of Dysfunctional Attitudes of victim vs. non-victim test groups in case of the boys.

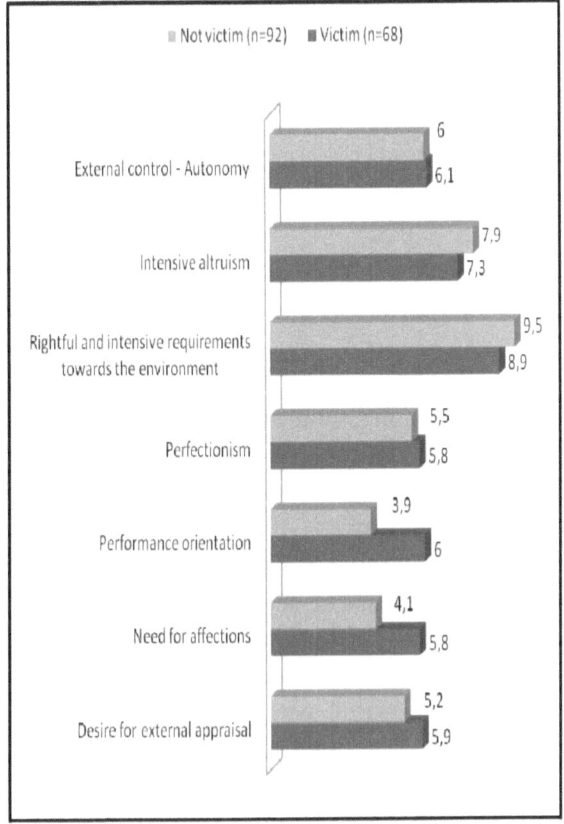

Figure 8. Averages Achieved on the Scale of Dysfunctional Attitudes by the Victim Test Group vs. Non-Victim Test Group (boys)

Comparative Statistical Analysis shows that there were significant differences between the test groups in point of only two dysfunctional attitudes.

These are the following:

> Performance orientation (t=3,217, p<0,002)
> Need for affections (t=2,918, p<0,005)

These results indicate that performance orientation, need for affections were rather typical of the boys becoming victims of school bullying than the boys not becoming victims.

The connection between the certain behavior patterns of school bullying and the dysfunctional attitudes was revealed by linear regression analysis (stepwise method: dependant variable was the certain behavior patterns, dysfunctional attitudes were used as predictors).

Chart 9 shows the results of linear regression analysis in case of victim behavior pattern.

In case of the girls, victim behavior pattern, from the dysfunctional attitudes, showed a significant, positive connection with need for affections and performance orientation, which together explained 6,8 % of the variance.

Predictor	B	t	P<
Women: $F_{totál}$=14,298; df=2/397; p<0,000			
Need for affections	0,155	2,811	0,005
Performance orientation	0,148	2,612	0,007
Men: $F_{totál}$=8,246; df=2/309; p<0,000			
Performance orientation	0,190	3,290	0,001
Rightful and intensive requirements towards the environment	-0,183	-3,164	0,002

Chart 9. Correlation between the Attitudes that Might Become Dysfunctional with the Victim Behaviour Pattern (approved models; p<0.05)

In case of the boys, victim behavior pattern, from the dysfunctional attitudes, showed a significant, positive connection with also performance orientation and a negative one with intensive requirements towards the environment , which together explained 5,1 % of the variance of victim behavior pattern.

We also examined that what the

connection is between the certain components of victim behavior pattern (cognitive, affective, physical reaction, lack of social support) and the dysfunctional attitudes (linear regression, stepwise method: dependant variable is the components of victim behavior pattern, dysfunctional attitudes were used as predictors).

Chart 10 shows the revealed connections with this method.

Predictor	B	t	P<
Cognitive (apperception and assimilation of the insult)			
Women: $F_{totál}$=7,347; df=1/397; p<0,007			
Need for affections	0,135	2,711	0,007
Men: $F_{totál}$=7,342; df=2/309; p<0,001			
Rightful and intensive requirements towards the environment	-0,192	-3,316	0,001
Performance orientation	0,158	2,727	0,007
Affective (emotional effect of the insult)			
Women: $F_{totál}$=26,407; df=2/397; p<0,000			
Need for affections	0,176	3,216	0,001
Performance orientation	0,158	2,891	0,004
Physical reaction (bodily reaction to the insult)			
Women: $F_{totál}$=9,974; df=1/397; p<0,002			
External control -	0,157	3,158	0,002

Autonomy			
Men: $F_{totál}$=11,394; df=2/309; p<0,000			
Performance orientation	0,171	2,862	0,005
Desire for external appraisal	0,146	2,452	0,015

Chart 10. Regression Analysis of the Attitudes that Might Become Dysfunctional Versus the Individual Components of the Victim Behaviour Pattern (approved models; p<0.05)

In case of the girls, the cognitive component of victim behavior pattern, from the dysfunctional attitudes, showed a significant, positive connection with need for affections and performance orientation, which together explained 1,8 % of the variance.

In case of the boys, the cognitive component of victim behavior pattern, from the dysfunctional attitudes, showed a significant, positive connection with performance orientation and a negative one with intensive requirements towards the environment , which together explained 4,6 % of the variance.

In case of the girls, the affective component of victim behavior pattern, from the dysfunctional attitudes, showed a significant, positive connection with need for affections and performance orientation, which together explained 8,2 % of the variance.

In case of the boys, the affective component of victim behavior pattern, from the dysfunctional attitudes, showed a significant, positive connection with neither of the attitudes.

In case of the girls, the physical reaction component of victim behavior pattern, from the dysfunctional attitudes, showed a significant, positive connection with external control attitude, which together explained 2,5 % of the variance.

In case of the boys, the physical reaction component of victim behavior pattern, from the dysfunctional attitudes, showed a significant, positive connection with performance orientation and desire for external appraisal, which together explained 6,9 % of the variance.

Lack of social support component of victim behavior pattern did not show significant, positive connection with any of the dysfunctional attitudes (Neither in case of the boys nor in case of the girls).

Coping Mechanisms

We examined what differences exist between the test groups in point of coping strategies on the basis of the results scored on the scales of the victim behavior pattern Questionnaire on School Bullying.

Figure 9 shows the averages scored on the certain scales of Conflict Solving Inventory of victim vs. non-victim test groups in case of the girls.

Comparative Statistical Analysis (two-sample t-test) shows that there were significant differences between the test groups in point of more coping strategies.

These are the following:

> Emotion focused coping strategy ($t=4,688$, $p<0,000$)
> Retrieval ($t=4,651$, $p<0,000$)
> Seeking emotional balance ($t=3,673$, $p<0,001$)
> Conformance ($t=2,673$, $p<0,008$)

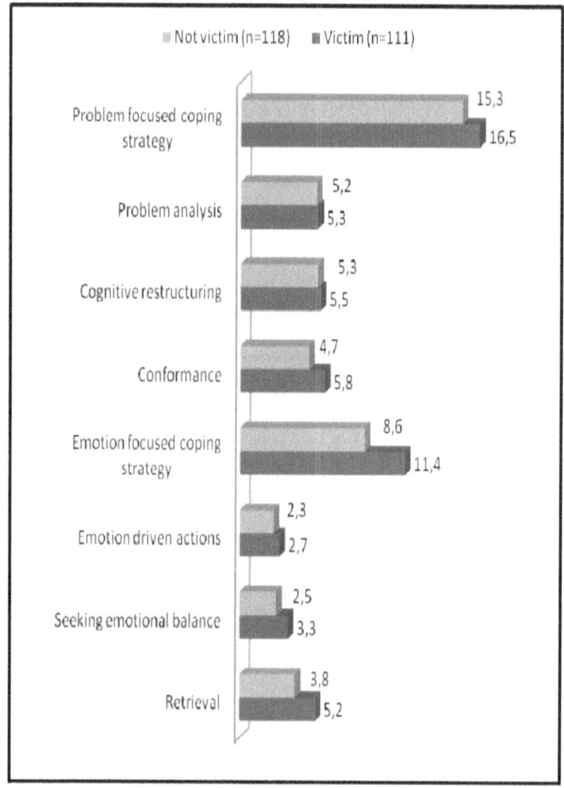

Figure 9. Averages Achieved on the Individual Scales of the Conflict Solving Inventory by the Victim Test Group vs. Non-Victim Test group (girls)

These results indicate that the emotion focused coping strategies especially retrieval and seeking emotional balance were rather typical of the girls becoming victims of school bullying. From the problem focused coping strategies, conformance was typical of them.

Figure 10 shows the averages scored on the certain scales of Conflict Solving Inventory of victim vs. non-victim test groups in case of the boys.

Comparative Statistical Analysis shows that there were significant differences between the test groups in point of only two coping strategies.

These are the following:

- Retrieval (t=2,448, p<0,016)
- Emotion focused coping strategy (t=2,098, p<0,038)

These results indicate that the emotion focused coping strategies especially retrieval was rather typical of the boys becoming victims of school bullying.

The connection between the victim behavior pattern of school bullying and the coping strategies was revealed by linear regression analysis (stepwise method: dependant variable was the victim behavior pattern, coping strategies were used as predictors).

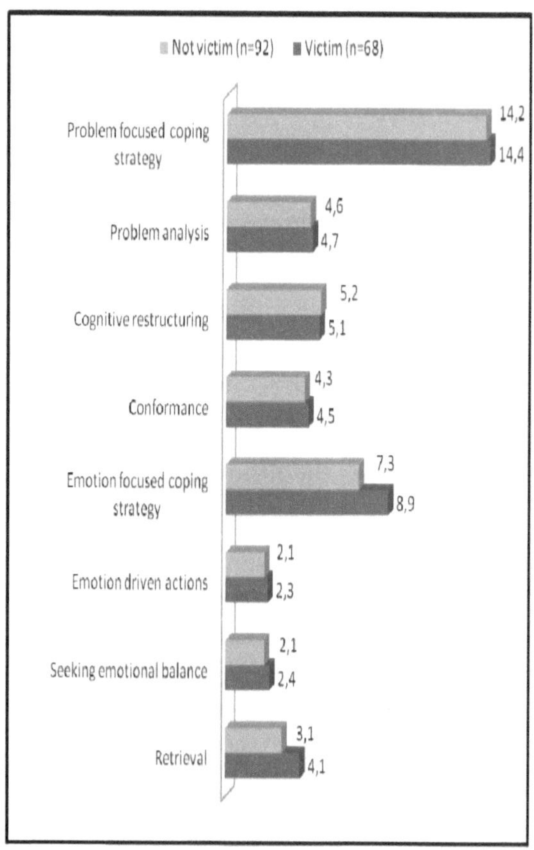

Figure 10. Averages Achieved on the Individual Scales of the Conflict Solving Inventory by the Victim Test Group vs. Non-Victim Test group (boys)

Chart 11 shows the results of linear regression analysis in case of victim behavior pattern.

Predictor	B	t	P<
Women: $F_{totál}$=13,157; df=2/397; p<0,000			
Retrieval	0,157	2,872	0,004
Conformance	0,137	2,503	0,013
Men: $F_{totál}$=10,794; df=2/309; p<0,000			
Retrieval	0,262	4,347	0,000
Cognitive restructuring	-0,165	-3,242	0,001

Chart 11. Correlation of Conflict Solving Strategies with the Victim Behaviour Pattern (approved models; p<0.05)

In case of the girls, victim behavior pattern, from the coping strategies, showed a significant, positive connection with retrieval and conformance, which together explained 6,3 % of the variance.

In case of the boys, victim behavior pattern, from the coping strategies, showed a significant, positive connection also with retrieval and a negative one with cognitive restructuring, which together explained 6,7 % of the variance.

We also examined that what the connection is between the certain components of victim behavior pattern (cognitive, affective, physical reaction, lack of social support) and the coping strategies (linear regression, stepwise method: dependant variable is the components of victim behavior pattern, coping strategies were used as predictors).

Chart 12 shows the revealed connections with this method.

Predictor	B	t	P<
Cognitive (apperception and assimilation of the insult)			
Women: $F_{totál}$=9,495; df=1/397; p<0,002			
Conformance	0,153	3,081	0,002
Men: $F_{totál}$=9,290; df=2/309; p<0,000			
Cognitive restructuring	-232	-3,835	0,000
Retrieval	0,202	3,337	0,001
Affective (emotional effect of the insult)			
Women: $F_{totál}$=27,836; df=1/397; p<0,000			
Retrieval	0,257	5,276	0,000
Men: $F_{totál}$=11,935; df=2/309; p<0,000			
Retrieval	0,293	4,882	0,000
Cognitive restructuring	-0,127	-2,118	0,035
Physical reaction (bodily reaction to the insult)			
Women: $F_{totál}$=22,683; df=1/397; p<0,000			
Emotion driven actions	0,233	4,763	0,000
Men: $F_{totál}$=52,343; df=1/309; p<0,000			
Emotion driven	0,382	7,235	0,000

actions			
Shortage of social support (refusal in the class community)			
Women: $F_{totál}$=4,102; df=1/397; p<0,017			
Problem analysis	-0,119	-2,245	0,017
Men: $F_{totál}$=7,613; df=1/309; p<0,006			
Problem analysis	-0,156	-2,759	0,006

Chart 12. Regression Analysis of Conflict Solving Strategies Versus the Individual Components of the Victim Behaviour Pattern (approved models; p<0.05)

In case of the girls, the cognitive component of victim behavior pattern, from the coping strategies, showed a significant, positive connection with conformance, which together explained 2,3 % of the variance.

In case of the boys, the cognitive component of victim behavior pattern, from the coping strategies, showed a significant, positive connection with retrieval and a negative one with cognitive restructuring, which together explained 3,7 % of the variance of victim behavior pattern.

In case of the girls, the affective component of victim behavior pattern, from the coping strategies, showed a significant, positive connection only with retrieval, which together explained 6,7 % of the variance.

In case of the boys, the affective component of victim behavior pattern, from the coping strategies, showed a significant, positive connection with retrieval and a negative one with cognitive restructuring, which together explained 7,2 % of the variance of victim behavior pattern.

In case of the girls, the physical reaction component of victim behavior pattern, from the coping strategies, showed a significant, positive connection only with emotion driven actions, which together explained 5,4 % of the variance.

In case of the boys, the physical reaction component of victim behavior pattern, from the coping strategies, showed a significant, positive connection also with emotion driven actions, which together explained 14,6 % of the variance.

In case of the girls, lack of social support component of victim behavior pattern, from the coping strategies, showed a significant, positive connection only with problem analysis, which explained 2,1 % of the variance.

In case of the boys, lack of social

support component of victim behavior pattern, from the coping strategies, showed a significant, positive connection also with problem analysis, which explained 2,4 % of the variance.

Discussion

Victim behavior pattern

In point of family socialization background effects, our research results show that conflict oriented family atmosphere –without reference to gender differences- may cause the appearance of the victim behavior pattern of school bullying.

Within this, the effect of conflict oriented family atmosphere (there are a lot of conflicts and quarrels in the family, things are not conducted) and the manipulative educational attitudes (parents manipulate the child emotionally) is strong., while the parents' behavior is inconsistent (the parents' behavior is unpredictable, making the child observe the rules depends on mood) as well as parental love and care is imperfect, parents do not give enough love and care.

Without reference to gender differences, rule oriented family atmosphere also causes the appearance of victim behavior pattern (there are strict rules in the family, which should be strictly kept, duties/obligations have been exactly divided up, everybody knows what to do). In addition, in case of the boys, the further samples of parental educational effects also cause the appearance of victim behavior pattern.

From the parental educational effects, we found parental overprotection the strongest, within this, the effect of maternal overprotection is strong. In case of the boys, parental restrictional behavior strategy associated with making an end of separateness calls forth victim behavior pattern as well.

Examining the temperament and character traits, we found that harm avoidance temperament trait and social unconcern character trait can be in the background of becoming victim (without reference to gender differences).

Narrowness, caution, tension, shyness, worry are typical of the harm avoidance types. In case of the girls becoming victims, these personality traits associate with social separateness, emotional coldness and/or emotional independence.

The most typical character trait of the victims was social unconcern. The character of the girls, who have become victims, was characterized by aimlessness and inadequacy and the lack responsibility and self-acceptance.

These research results confirm Rost's research results (1998), who found that victims are uncertain and shy. They also confirm Olweus'results (1997), who thinks that victims were characterized by a certain caution and sensitivity at an early age. These traits root on harm avoidance temperament traits.

Our research results, which examine emotions, attitudes and coping, show that the students, who become bullies through school bullying –without reference to gender differences-primarily, feel fear, which force them to retrieval. They cork up anger. Their performance orientation can be increased. Beside the above mentioned emotions: anger and retrieval, shame and conformance coping strategy can be typical of the girls, who become victims. They expect ideal but not real behavior from their environment and they suffer if they do not get it. In case of the boys, who became victims, contempt as well as inability to cognitive restructuring is appeared. In addition, intensive need for affections is also typical of them.

Bully-Victim behavior pattern

Researches examining the family background of provocative victims revealed that the harsh, negative behavior is very common in the provocative victims' families; the parents are often unable to control their emotions. The provocative victim type boys often have a close contact with their mother and a distant one with their father. The mother of the provocative victim type girls is rather hostile than overprotective (Révész, 2007).

In our research, in point of family socialization background effects, we could partly confirm the above mentioned results.

Conflict oriented family atmosphere, rule oriented family atmosphere, and parental overprotection can cause the appearance of the bully-victim behavior pattern (without reference to gender differences). In a conflict oriented family atmosphere, the lack of parental love and care, conflict oriented family atmosphere, which is associated with manipulative and inconsistent educational attitudes, make the child become the bully-victim victim of school bullying.

Children can be bully-victims in an overprotective family (especially in case of the boys) and rule oriented family.

Examining the temperament and character traits, we found that the background of becoming bully-victims was different in case of the two genders.

The most typical temperament trait of the bully-victim type girls was the lack of dependence on other people's acceptance. The lack of self-directedness and social intolerance were typical of their characters.

The bully-victim type boys' most typical temperament trait was harm-avoidance and their most typical character trait was apathy.

References

Cook C., Williams K., Guerra N, Kim T. (2009): Variability in the prevalence of bullying and victimization A cross-national and methodological analysis. In: Jimerson S, Swearer S, Espelage D, (Editors): *The international handbook of school bullying*. p. 347-362.

Duncan R. (1999): Maltreatment by parents and peers: The relationship between child abuse, bully victimization and psychological distress. *Child Maltreat*. 19:45-56.

Eslea M, Menesini E, Morita Y, O'Moore M, Mora-Merchan JA, Pereira B, et al. (2004): Friendship and loneliness among bullies and victims: Data from seven countries. *Aggressive Behavior*. 30 (1):71-83.

Figula E, Margitics F, Pauwlik Zs. (2019): *The Questionnaire on School Bullying /handbook/*. KeryPub. New York.

Giesekus, U. (2002). *Gewalt: die alltägliche Gefahr*. Wuppertal, Kassel: Oncken Verlag.

Goch, I. (1998). *Entwicklung der*

Ungewissheitstoleranz. Die Bedeutung der familialen Socialization. Regensburg: Roderer.

Hawker, D., Boulton, M. (2000). Twenty years' research on peer victimization and psychosocial maladjustment: A meta-analytic review of cross-sectional studies. *Journal of Child Psychology and Psychiatry*, 41(4), 441–455.

Hymel, S., Swearer, S. M. (2015). Four decades of research on school bullying: An introduction. *American Psychologist*, 70(4), 293–299.

Izard, C.E. (1971): *The Face of Emotions*. Appleton-Century-Crofts, New York.

Kathleen, R. (2007): *Bullying auf dem Schulweg: Das Schulbus-Phänomen. Erstellung eines Persönlichkeitsprofils von Tätern und Opfern. Eine empirische Studie in Thüringen. Dissertation zur Erlangung des academischen Grades doctor philosophiae* (Dr. phil.), Friedrich Schiller Universität Jena.

Kopp, M. (1994). *Orvosi pszichológia.* Budapest: SOTE Magatartástudományi Intézet.

Kopp, M., Skrabski Á. (1995). *Alkalmazott*

magatartástudomány. *[Applied behavioral science.]* Budapest: Corvinus Kiadó.

Lereya, S., Samara, M., Wolke, D. (2013). Parentingbehavior and the riskof becoming a victimand abully/victim: A meta-analysis study. *Child Abuse & Neglect*, 37, 1091–1108.

Margitics, F; Figula, E; Pauwlik, Zs (2010): *Temperamentum, karakter és iskolai erőszak.* Nyíregyháza, Élmény '94 Bt.142 p.

Margitics, F; Figula, E; Pauwlik, Zs (2010): *Prevalence of School Bullying in Hungarian Primary and High Schools.* KeryPub. New York.

Olweus, D. (1978). *Aggression in the schools: Bullies and whipping boys.* Washington, DC: Hemisphere (Wiley).

Olweus, D. (1993): Bully/victim problems among school children: Long-term consequences and an effective intervention program. In S. Hodhings (Ed.), *Mental disorder and crime,* (pp. 317- 349). Thousand Oaks, CA: Sage Publications.

Olweus, D. (1997). Täter-Opfer-Probleme in der Schule: Erkenntnisstand und Interventionsprogramm. In: Holtappels, H. G.; Heitmeyer, W.;

Melzer, W.; Tillmann, K.-J. *Forschung über Gewalt an Schulen. Erscheinungsformen und Ursachen, Konzepte und Prävention.* Weinheim, München: Juventa Verlag.

Olweus, D. (2010). Understanding and researching bullying: Some critical issues. In Jimerson, S. Swearer, S. Espelage, D. (Eds.), *Handbook of bullying in schools: An international perspective* (pp. 9–33). New York: Routledge.

Olweus D., Breivik K. (2014): Plight of Victims of School Bullying: The Opposite of Well-Being. In. Ben-Arieh A. et al. (eds.), *Handbook of Child Well-Being,* Springer Science+Business Media, Dordrecht.

Oláh, A. (2005): *Érzelmek, megküzdés és optimális élmény.* Trefor Kiadó, Budapest.

Révész Gy. (2007): Erőszak az iskolában In. Péley B., Révész Gy. (szerk): *Autonómia és identitás. Tanulmányok Kézdi Balázs 70. születésnapjára.* Pannónia Könyvek, Pécs, 162-179.

Rost, D. (1998). *Handbuch Pädagogische Psychologie.* Weinheim: Beltz Verlag.

Rózsa S., Kállai, J., Osváth, A., Bánki M. Cs. (2005). *Temperamentum és karakter:*

Cloninger pszichobiológiai modellje. A Cloninger-féle temperamentum és karakter kérdőív felhasználói kézikönyve. Budapest: Medicina Könyvkiadó Rt.

Sallay, H., Dabert, C. (2002). Women's perception of parenting: a German-Hungarian comparison. *Applied Psychology in Hungary, 3-4*, 55-56.

Salmivalli, C., Nieminen, E. (2002). Proactive and reactive aggression among school bullies, victims, and bully victims. *Aggressive Behavior*, 28, 30–44.

Schwartz, D. (2000). Subtypes of victims and aggressors in children's peer groups. *Journal of Abnormal Child Psychology*, 28, 181–192.

Smith, P., Madsen, K., Moody, K.. (1999): What causes the age decline in reports of being bullied at school? Toward a developmental analysis of risks of being bullied. *Educational Research, 41,* 267-285.

Solberg, M., Olweus, D., Endresen, I. (2007). Bullies and victims at school: Are they the same pupils? *British Journal of Educational Psychology,*

77, 441–464.

Swearer, S., Hymel, S. (2015). Understanding the psychology of bullying: Moving toward a socialecological diathesis–stress model. *American Psychologist*, 70 (4), 344–353.

Tóth, I., Gervai, J. (1999). Szülői Bánásmód Kérdőív (H-PBI): a Parental Bonding Instrument magyar változata. *Magyar Pszichológiai Szemle, 54*, 551-566.

Yang A., Salmivalli C. (2013) Different forms of bullying and victimization: Bully-victims versus bullies and victims, *European Journal of Developmental Psychology*, 10:6, 723-738.

Volk, A., Camilleri, J., Dane, A., Marini, Z. (2012). Is adolescent bullying an evolutionary adaptation? *Aggressive Behavior,* 38(3), 222–238.

Weisman, A., Beck, A.T. (1979). *The Dysfunctional Attitude Scale.* Thesis, University of Pennsylvania.

Wolke D, Woods S, Bloomfield L, Karstadt L. (2000): The association between direct and relational bullying and behaviour problems among primary school children. *J Child Psychol Psychiatry*. 41:989-1002.

Previous Publications

Look inside at Amazon.com
https://www.amazon.com/dp/B07XD2S48T

Look inside at Amazon.com
https://www.amazon.com/dp/B07YYNN4K2

Look inside at Amazon.com
https://www.amazon.com/dp/1706199848